The Count's

By RAY SIPHERD • Pictures by TOM COOKE

Featuring Jim Henson's Sesame Street Muppets

A SESAME STREET/GOLDEN PRESS BOOK

Published by Western Publishing Company, Inc., in cooperation with Children's Television Workshop. © 1978 Children's Television Workshop. Muppet characters © 1978 Muppets, Inc. All rights reserved. Printed in the U.S.A. No part of this book may be reproduced or copied in any form without written permission from the publisher. The Count is a trademark of Muppets, Inc. Sesame Street® and the Sesame Street sign are trademarks and service marks of Children's Television Workshop. GOLDEN®, A FIRST LITTLE GOLDEN BOOK, and GOLDEN PRESS® are registered trademarks of Western Publishing Company, Inc. Library of Congress Catalog Card Number: 81-83506 ISBN 0-307-10123-1 / ISBN 0-307-68123-8 (lib. bdg.) ABCDEFGHIJ

Counting can be lots of fun
When you start with number...

Next, the number that is due
Is the lovely number...

You are counting splendidly
If you count the number...

Don't stop now, but count some more!
Add a great big number...

To keep our counting game alive,
Next we count the number...

No Account Count

Now a hint: It's *not* eleven.
What comes next is number...

Very good! But don't be late.
Turn the page for number...

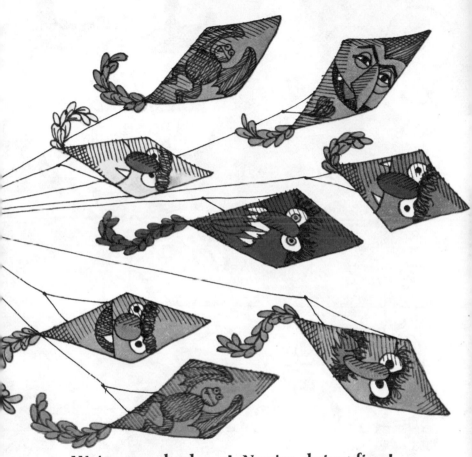

We're nearly done! You're doing fine!
Together now—the number...

And now our counting's ended when
We conclude with number...